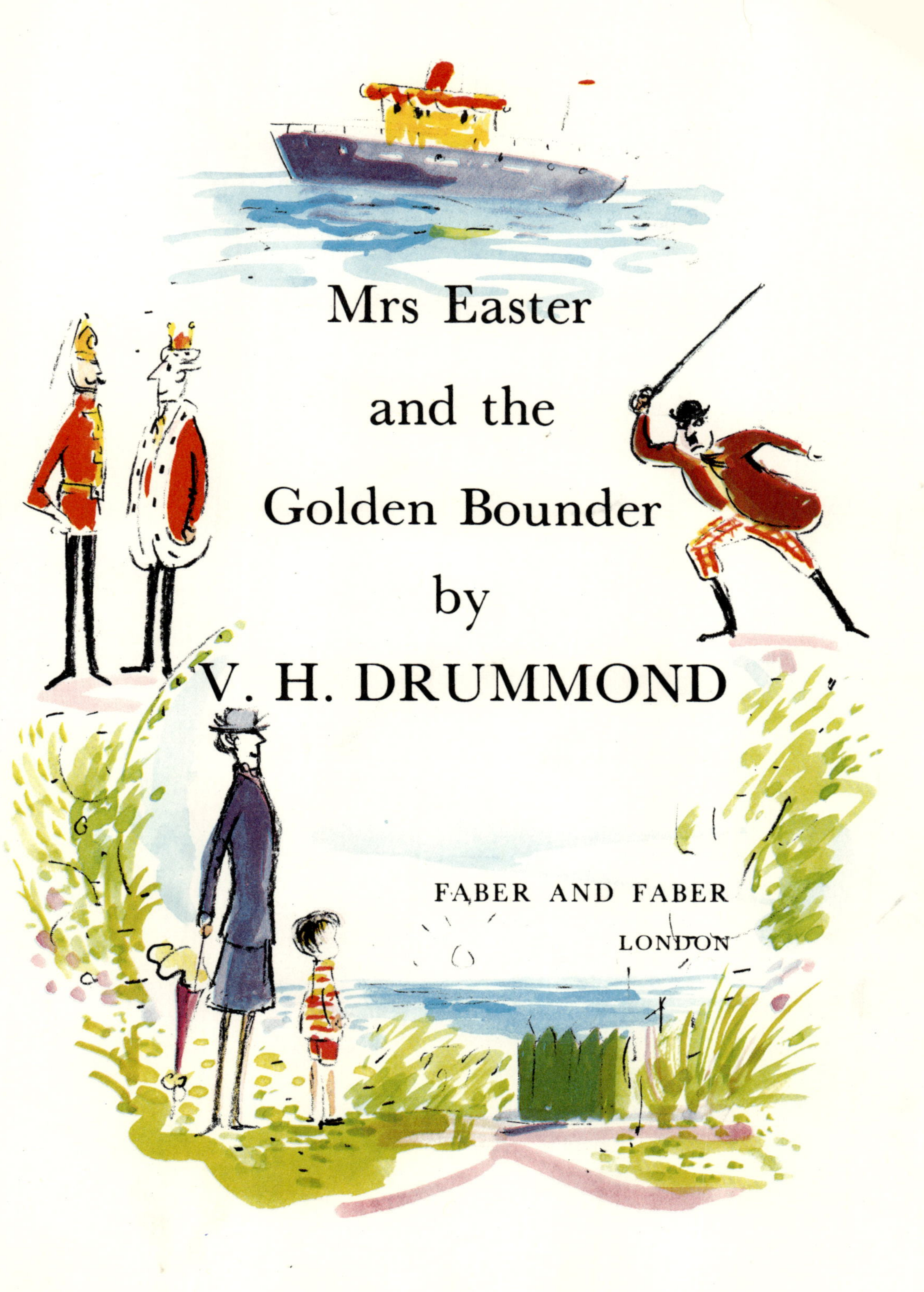

Mrs Easter and the Golden Bounder

by

V. H. DRUMMOND

FABER AND FABER

LONDON

First published in 1970
by Faber and Faber Limited
24 Russell Square London WC1
Printed in Great Britain by
Latimer Trend & Co. Ltd., Whitstable

SBN 571 08870 8

For
JOANNA

A long time ago an Admiral, Admiral Easter, sailed about the seas in a sailing ship, the *Golden Bounder*. Till one unfortunate day when the wind blew the *Bounder* over and it sank to the bottom of the sea.

"Well, that's that," said the Admiral as he swam ashore. "I'll go no more a-roving."

So he built himself a house on the cliff-top, with some steps leading up from the beach. And there he spent the rest of his days.

Then for hundreds of years his descendants lived in it, until it came into the possession of Mrs. Easter, Billie Guftie's aunt.

One day when Billie Guftie was staying with Mrs. Easter she said to him:

"Alas. I fear I cannot afford to go on living here. I shall have to move to a small flat."

Together they looked up at the picture of Admiral Easter and the *Golden Bounder* and they both felt very sad.

"But come," said Mrs. Easter. "We must not mope. Let's go down to the beach."

They walked to the little gate that opened on to the steps that led to the beach.

"The sun is hot," said Mrs. Easter and put up her parasol. But at that moment a gust of wind came and blew her off her feet!

"Oh my dearest Aunt ... come back, come back!" cried Billie Guftie, grabbing her coat. But another gust of wind came and blew them both right over the cliff ... over the deep sea!

"Are you still there, Billie Guftie" enquired Mrs. Easter, as the wind blew them further and further from the shore.

"Yes," said Billie Guftie.

Just then they noticed what looked like a tiny boat far below, but as they got nearer they saw it was a fine yacht.

"Look at the flag!" cried Mrs. Easter. "It must be the Royal Yacht."

And, sure enough, there was the King strolling on the deck with his bodyguard Sir Archie Argyle. When the King saw them he waved graciously.

"Would you care to come aboard my yacht?" he called.

"Oh yes, Your Majesty," replied Mrs. Easter.

"Then please descend," said the King.

Mrs. Easter carefully closed her parasol and made a perfect landing on the deck of the Royal Yacht.

"Were you going anywhere in particular?" asked the King.

"Oh no," replied Mrs. Easter. "We were just blown off the cliffs by mistake."

"Then we can take you back to the shore," said the King.

While Mrs. Easter and the King sat on the deck and talked, Sir Archie showed Billie Guftie round the yacht. Then he lent him his telescope. Billie Guftie could see for miles through the telescope, even as far as Mrs. Easter's house. He noticed a strange-looking figure moving mysteriously about amongst the rocks below the house.

He gave the telescope back to Sir Archie, who raised it to his eye.

"It's Vilewort the Villain," he exclaimed excitedly. "Wearing a diving outfit and fishy flippered feet!"

"Vilewort the Villain!" echoed the King. "He's up to no good, I'm sure!"

"He's just dived into the sea," cried Sir Archie.

"Rev up the engines," ordered the King. "We must hurry and find out what villainy Vilewort is up to!"

When they got to the spot where Vilewort was last seen, there was no trace of him.

"I think I should go down and see what he's doing," said Sir Archie.

"You'd better put on your diving suit or you'll get frightfully wet," said the King.

"Can I come with you, Sir Archie?" asked Billie Guftie, eagerly.

Mrs. Easter looked doubtful.

"It's quite safe, Mrs. Easter," said the King. "They will be tied securely to these." He pointed to two large spools with ropes and handles.

So Sir Archie and Billie Guftie dressed up in diving gear of close-fitting plastic with special transparent helmets for breathing under water.

Then they were tied to the two spools and let down into the sea. The King turned the handle of one spool and Mrs. Easter turned the other.

Billie Guftie felt quite warm in his plastic suit.

There was no sign of Vilewort on the ocean bed. Sir Archie got out his walky-talky to report to the King.

"Ocean Bed to Royal Yacht," he said. "No sign of villain . . . over!"

"Royal Yacht to Ocean Bed," came the reply from the King. "Search about . . . we are with you."

"Message understood," said Sir Archie. Then he told Billie Guftie to swim after him and keep his eyes open for Vilewort.

Billie Guftie enjoyed swimming under the sea and looking at the strange fishes, shells and sea plants.

Everything seemed wonderful till suddenly a huge swordfish, a creature with a fearful spike sticking out of the front of its face, emerged from under a dark rock and advanced menacingly towards them. Billie Guftie was very frightened but Sir Archie drew his sword and a tremendous fight began. The great fish parried skilfully but Sir Archie's superior swordmanship won the battle and it went off in a huff.

They swam on till they came to the wreck of a huge ship. Amongst the barnacles and seaweed that covered it some carved words could be faintly seen.

Sir Archie spelt them out.

"T-H-E G-O-L-D-E-N B-O-U-N-D-E-R."

"The *Golden Bounder!*" gasped Billie Guftie. "It must be the wreck of Admiral Easter's ship."

It was dark and slippery amongst the rotten planks of the wreck. Billie Guftie groped about until suddenly, in the dim light, he saw a rusty old chest.

At that moment he heard a scuffling and a splashing and looking up he saw, peering over the side of the wreck, the ugly face of Vilewort the Villain!

"Ha, ha! he, he! The treasure!" cried Vilewort.

Billie Guftie ran towards the chest.

"Leave it alone, boy . . . I want it!" shouted Vilewort. He seized an ancient sword lying nearby and, with a vicious thrust, cut the rope that attached Billie Guftie to the Royal Yacht.

Sir Archie came hurrying up.

"Be off with you, Vilewort," he shouted, brandishing his sword at him. Then a terrible fight took place. Round and round the deck they pranced and lunged.

Till Vilewort shouted:

"Cricker crick! Cricker cree! You can't catch me!" and took a mighty swipe at Sir Archie's rope, but Sir Archie parried just in time and knocked Vilewort head over heels.

The voice of the monarch was heard from above, saying:

"What's going on down there?"

Sir Archie grasped the chest and Billie Guftie held on to his rope.

"Kindly pull us up, your Majesty," gasped Sir Archie, into the walky talky, and they began slowly to rise.

"My!" groaned the King. "Archie seems to have got much heavier!"

But Mrs. Easter had the fright of her life when she pulled up her rope and there was no Billie Guftie attached to it.

"Oh my darling nephew," she cried in despair. "He is lost at the bottom of the sea."

But at that moment the King, with a tremendous tug, managed to pull up Sir Archie Argyle, Billie Guftie and the weighty chest. Sir Archie heaved the chest on to the deck, then he handed Billie Guftie into Mrs. Easter's arms.

Meanwhile Vilewort the Villain had been following them in a last desperate effort to capture the treasure chest.

Imagine his surprise and embarrassment when he surfaced and found himself face to face with the King!

"Vilewort tried to steal the treasure," said Sir Archie.

"Then as a punishment you must swim to the shore," said the King. "I won't have villains like you aboard my yacht."

Then the King said:

"Well, now let's see what's inside this chest."

It was so rusty they had great difficulty in opening it. But when, at last, they succeeded they all gasped! For it was absolutely full of golden coins!

"No wonder it was so heavy," said the King.

"It's treasure trove," said Sir Archie. "Therefore it belongs to the King!"

"I don't want it, I've got plenty of money," said the King. "I think Mrs. Easter should have it, as it belonged to her ancestor Admiral Easter."

Mrs. Easter thanked him. She could hardly believe her good fortune.

"This is indeed a windfall!" she exclaimed. "Now I shall be able to live for ever in the house on the cliff-top!"

Then the King invited them all into the state cabin for tea. There were chocolate biscuits, savoury sandwiches, and buns called matelot-hats that had white icing and a cherry on top.

As they drifted towards the shore they passed Vilewort swimming along, looking extremely cross.

When they got to the beach Mrs. Easter and Billie Guftie thanked the King and Sir Archie for a very pleasant afternoon and Sir Archie helped them up the cliff steps with the treasure chest.

Mrs. Easter waved her parasol as the Royal Yacht disappeared over the horizon.

THE END